TITANIC
TRIVIA

Compiled by David Downs
and
Ken Beck

PREMIUM PRESS AMERICA
NASHVILLE, TENNESSEE

TITANIC TRIVIA by David Downs and Ken Beck
Published by PREMIUM PRESS AMERICA
Copyright © 1998 by David Downs and Ken Beck

ISBN 1-887654-42-9

Library of Congress Catalog Card Number 98-66159

PREMIUM PRESS AMERICA books are available at special discounts for premiums, sales promotions, fund-raising, or educational use. For details contact the Publisher at P.O. Box 159015, Nashville, TN 37215, or phone toll free (800) 891-7323 or (615) 256-8484.

Cover & interior by Bob Bubnis/BookSetters
Cover photo from the collection of Eric Daily
Printed by FALCON PRESS

First Edition 1998
3 4 5 6 7 8 9 10

Introduction

It was claimed "the unsinkable" but in the end it proved to be the unthinkable. After the *Titanic* went down in the early hours of April 15, 1912, news of the greatest sea calamity of all time hit the rest of the world like a brick hurricane.

Now some 86 years later, tales of the *Titanic* continue to astonish and tantalize the curious along with the truth seekers and many others who find themselves wanting to know more about the world's most unfathomable accident.

Who can explain the *Titanic's* stronghold on man's imagination? The ship was the first and the biggest and the last of its kind. And its human cargo included the wealthiest men and women on earth, along with hundreds of immigrants who had little more than the clothes on their backs and a suitcase full of possessions.

That maiden voyage never reached safe harbor as it met its fateful end, but man's fascination for the *Titanic* has proven to be neverending.

This never-before-published photo from the private collection of Eric Daily shows the *Titanic* being tugged out of Belfast Harbor as it prepares to set off to Southampton to pick up its first load of passengers.

1. "Iceberg right ahead!"—Frederick Fleet, at 11:40 p.m. on April 14, 1912.

2. In the 1898 novel *Futility,* 14 years before the sinking of the *Titanic*, Morgan Robertson penned a fictitious tale about a ship named the *Titan* which rams an iceberg and sinks with many victims. Some of the uncanny similarities between the book and the *Titanic* calamity include the month (April), the length of the ship (*Titanic*, 882 feet; *Titan,* 800 feet), and the number of passengers on board (*Titanic*, 2,200; *Titan*, 2,000).

3. In April of 2002, on the 90th anniversary of her maiden voyage, the *Titanic* will get a second chance to make the trip to New York. A swiss-based company is building a $500 million dollar full size replica of the luxury liner and is planning to sell tickets ranging from $10,000–$100,000 each. This one, however, will come with modern iceberg detecting equipment.

4. The *Titanic* had four funnels that were 22 feet in diameter and 62 feet tall. The fourth funnel, known as a dummy funnel, was added for appearance sake and also served as a kitchen ventilator.

5. Measuring 882 feet and 9 inches long, and 92 feet and 6 inches wide, and weighing 46,328 tons, the *Titanic* was the largest ship ever built prior to 1912.

6. It cost $7.5 million to build the *Titanic*, while *Titanic*, the 1997 movie, cost $200 million to make. The *Titanic* carried an $5 million insurance policy. It would cost about $400 million to build the *Titanic* today.

7. A 1943 Nazi propaganda film, directed by Herbert Selpin and orchestrated by Nazi propaganda chief Josef Goebbels, featured a fictional sole German on board as the hero.

8. The *Titanic* featured a dog kennel for the passengers' pets. One of the crewman walked the dogs daily along the decks.

9. The original plans for the *Titanic* were sketched on a napkin by J. Bruce Ismay.

10. Director James Cameron (*The Terminator, Aliens, The Abyss,* and *True Lies*) vowed not to make the 1997 film *Titanic* unless he could dive to the actual wreck.

11. The *Titanic's* original maiden voyage date, March 20, 1912, was rescheduled due to the collision that *Titanic's* sister ship the *Olympic* had with the *Hawke* on September 20, 1911, which put construction on the *Titanic*, which was in drydock, on hold until the *Olympic* could be repaired. Commanding the *Olympic* at the time of this collision was Captain Edward J. Smith.

12. The *Titanic* carried 11,000 pounds of fresh fish, 75,000 pounds of fresh meat, 180 boxes or 36,000 oranges, 1,500 bottles of wine, and 20,000 bottles of beer and stout.

13. The *Titanic* struck an iceberg at 11:40 p.m. April 14, 1912. The mighty vessel sank less than three hours later at 2:20 a.m. April 15.

14. A passenger freed all the dogs from the *Titanic* kennel, but only two survived after their owners found places in the lifeboats for them.

15. How many people were aboard the *Titanic* for her maiden voyage? The best estimate is 1,316 passengers, including 606 in the cabin classes and 710 in steerage, and 892 crew members, totaling 2,208 on the *Titanic* when she left Queenstown, Ireland, for New York.

16. Chief Officer Henry T. Wilde wrote a letter to his sister, while serving on the *Titanic*, that said, "I still don't like this ship. I have a queer feeling about it."

17. The maiden voyage of the *Titanic* was the last command of Captain Edward J. Smith before he planned to retire at age 62. Smith had sailed over two million miles with the White Star Line over a 30–year span.

18. Thanks to the tugboat *Vulcan* and Captain Edward J. Smith's quick reactions, the *Titanic* narrowly avoided a collision with the American liner *New York* when *Titanic* departed Southampton Harbour April 10, 1912.

19. Fourth Officer Boxhall noted in the log that as the *Titanic* left Cherbourg, France, for the open sea that no sea gulls were following the ship. He wrote down "how queer."

20. The *Olympic*, *Titanic*, and *Britannic* were built by Harland & Wolff on a 220-foot-high-gantry, the largest in the world, to accommodate the massive size of the new fleet of White Star liners.

21. While stopping in Queenstown, Ireland, an odd occurrence caused some *Titanic* passengers to believe that this incident was a premonition of the danger that lay ahead. During this stopover, the blackened face of a stoker was seen peering out of the top of the fourth funnel.

22. John George Phillips, 24, Chief Wireless Operator on board the *Titanic*, made a salary of about $20 a month. He died with the ship.

23. The net worth of the wealthiest men and women aboard the *Titanic* has been estimated at about $250 million.

24. "I feel that if research and salvage of the *Titanic* will benefit all people, then such activities should be encouraged." —*Titanic* survivor Louis Kink Pope to the United States Senate concerning the excavation of artifacts from the *Titanic*.

25. On March 14, 1998, *Titanic* (1997) became the best-selling box-office film in U.S. history as it surpassed *Star Wars'* mark of $461 million. Worldwide, *Titanic* has sold more than $1.1 billion in tickets and is still going strong.

26. Alfred Hitchcock had planned to make a film about the *Titanic* as his first American film in 1938. "They (cruise-line operators) seem to think that if I recapture all the horror and violence of the situation, it will stop people going on cruises," the master of suspense told an interviewer. He never made the film.

27. "The *Titanic* itself lies in 13,000 feet of water on a gently sloping alpine-like countryside overlooking a small canyon below. Its bow faces north and the ship sits upright on the bottom. Its mighty stacks point upward. There is no light at this great depth and little light can be found. It is quiet and peaceful and a fitting place for the remains of this greatest of sea tragedies to rest. May it forever remain that way and may God bless these found souls."—Robert D. Ballard's Washington, D.C., press conference after returning from the North Atlantic after discovering the *Titanic's* final resting place on September 1, 1985.

28. It took six anchor chains and two piles of cable-dragging chains, weighing 80 tons each, to stop the *Titanic*, which was traveling at 12 knots when she was launched. The entire launching process took just 62 seconds.

29. Starring Tim Curry as a steward, George C. Scott as Captain Edward John Smith, and Scott Hylands as John Jacob Astor, CBS broadcast a four-hour TV miniseries titled *Titanic* in November 1996.

30. Originally named the Titanic Enthusiasts of America, the Titanic Historical Society, Inc., was founded at the home of Edward S. Kamuda on September 6, 1963, in Indian Orchard, Massachusetts.

31. Every year on the anniversary of the *Titanic's* sinking, April 15, the United States Coast Guard drops a wreath over the *Titanic's* last radio position in memory of those who lost their lives.

32. The *Titanic* took a full 10 months to fit out from the time she was launched on May 31, 1911, until the day she departed for New York.

33. *A Night To Remember* by Walter Lord is the most complete account of the *Titanic* tragedy. Author Lord interviewed 60 survivors of the *Titanic* for his 1955 book. In 1986 Lord wrote *The Night Lives On,* as he added more facts and laid to rest old legends.

34. Noted philanthropist and co-owner of the Macy's department store in New York, Isidor Straus and his wife Ida occupied stateroom C55. Straus was worth a reported $20 million at the time of his death.

35. On April 2, 1912, the *Titanic* began her trials after being escorted into the Victoria Channel by four tugboats, the *Hornby, Herald, Herculaneum,* and the *Huskisson.* The four tugs accompanied *Titanic* into Belfast Lough where, under her own power, *Titanic* sailed to Southampton to make ready for her maiden voyage.

36. The great ship was never christened, but 23 tons of soft soap, train oil and tallow were used to launch the *R.M.S. Titanic* at 12:13 p.m. May 31, 1911. The *R.M.S.* stands for Royal Mail Steamer.

37. Among the legends that materialized about the *Olympic* and *Titanic* were that there was a golf course on board and that a herd of dairy cows was on board to supply the milk to the passengers. The *Titanic* did carry 1,500 gallons of fresh milk.

38. There were four elevators on the *Titanic*: three were used to take passengers into areas located on A, B, C, or D Decks and the fourth was to transfer passengers from G Deck to the Boat Deck.

39. Never did the White Star Line ads for the *Titanic* use the word "unsinkable."

40. Not a single lifeboat drill was ever conducted during the *Titanic's* voyage.

41. Railway and shipping magnate George W. Vanderbilt on April 9, 1912, the day before the *Titanic's* scheduled departure, canceled his booking on the *Titanic* after his mother convinced him that maiden voyages were too troublesome.

42. To furnish the many beds that *Titanic* passengers and crew would sleep on, the *Titanic* carried 3,600 bed covers, 800 eiderdown quilts, 15,000 single sheets, 3,000 double sheets, and 15,000 pillow-slips.

43. Half a million rivets, weighing 270 tons, were used to build the bottom of the *Titanic* alone, comprising only one-sixth of the amount needed to construct the whole ship.

44. Second-class passenger Esther Hart, who survived the *Titanic* disaster along with her daughter Eva, stayed up each night she was on the *Titanic* and slept during the day because she was convinced that the "unsinkable" label given the *Titanic* was a premonition of disaster. She only left her cabin for meals.

45. It took a team of 20 horses to pull one of the 15-and-a-half-ton anchors on the *Titanic*.

46. The workers that built the *Titanic* worked 49-hour weeks and were paid about $10 a week.

47. While briefly docking in Queenstown, Ireland, seven passengers disembarked from the *Titanic*, including Father Francis Browne, who took the only known photographs of life aboard the *Titanic* before her fateful voyage into history.

48. Two of the *Titanic's* millionaire suites contained private promenade decks.

49. John Jacob Astor and his wife paid close to $4,000 for the suite they occupied on the *Titanic*, which was one of the most elegant and lavish. Today, a similar suite would cost $50,000.

50. Hollywood's 1953 film account of the sea disaster, titled *Titanic*, starred Robert Wagner, Clifton Webb, Barbara Stanwyck, and Richard Basehart (who, ironically, 11 years later starred in the TV series *Voyage to the Bottom of the Sea*). The script won an Oscar.

51. Before sailing to New York, the *Titanic* stopped in Queenstown, Ireland, to pick up 120 third-class passengers, seven second-class passengers, and 1,385 sacks of mail.

52. The bottled beer on the *Titanic* was supplied by Charles George Hibbert & Co. of Southampton and London. The company was so honored to supply the *Titanic* with bottled beer that it printed special posters reading "Bottled Beer for the White Star liner *Titanic*, the Largest Vessel in the World" to promote their product.

53. Initially the order of officers had William Murdoch as Chief Officer, Charles Lightoller as First Officer, and David Blair as Second Officer. White Star Line then decided to assign Henry Wilde to the *Titanic* as Chief Officer, bumping Murdoch to First Officer and Lightoller to Second Officer. Blair was reassigned to another ship.

54. There were more than 3,560 cork lifebelts on the *Titanic*.

55. The *Titanic* featured four parlour suites for the first-class passengers. These staterooms consisted of a sitting room, two bedrooms, two wardrobe rooms, a private bath, and a lavatory.

56. The fee to send a wireless message from the *Titanic* was a minimum of $3.12 for 10 words, and 35 cents for every other word.

57. The *Titanic* was 11 stories high and nearly four city blocks long.

58. In 1907 White Star Line chairman J. Bruce Ismay met with the head of Harland & Wolff, Lord Pirrie, to plan the construction of three new gigantic liners, the *Olympic*, *Titanic*, and *Gigantic* (later named *Britannic*). The only ship of those three sister ships that did not sink was the *Olympic*.

59. Frederick Wheeler, the servant of George W. Vanderbilt, still sailed on the *Titanic* to accompany the Vanderbilt's luggage, even though his employers canceled at the last minute, and was one of the ship's victims.

60. The ultra-modern squash court on the *Titanic* was 30 feet long and 20 feet wide.

61. Captain E.J. Smith received a variety of medals and honors for serving in the Boer War, including the Transport Medal, The Reserve Decoration, and the rank of Commander in the Royal Naval Reserve, which distinguished the ships commanded by him because being part of the Royal Naval Reserve meant that their masters could fly the "Blue Duster" of the Royal Naval Reserve. The "Blue Duster" was raised on the stern flagpost of the *Titanic* on sailing day, April 10, 1912.

62. A steward would deliver the *Titanic's* own daily newspaper, *The Atlantic Daily Bulletin,* to the first-class passengers on their way to breakfast each morning.

63. Bugler P.W. Fletcher announced meals were to be served on the *Titanic* by performing *The Roast Beef of Old England.*

64. After hiding in a pile of mailbags, 24-year-old John Coffey deserted the crew of the *Titanic* at Queenstown, Ireland.

65. As the *Titanic* departed from Southampton on her maiden voyage, the tugboats *Neptune, Hector, Hercules, Vulcan, Albert Edward,* and *Ajax* all played a critical role in the *Titanic's* near collision with the liner *New York.*

66. Third-class accommodations on the *Titanic* rivaled the first-class quality found on most liners of the late 1800s and were far more elegant than most second- and third-class accommodations on other liners in 1912.

67. Directed by James Cameron, the 1997 film *Titanic* won 11 Oscars at the 1998 Academy Awards show: Best Picture, Best Director, Film Editing, Original Song, Dramatic Score, Art Direction, Cinematography, Visual Effects, Costume, Sound Effects Editing, Sound, and it tied the record for the most Oscars ever, sharing the honors with *Ben-Hur*.

68. A first-class ticket for a parlor suite on the *Titanic* cost $4,350, which would be about $50,000 in today's dollars. First-class tickets for a berth cost $150 ($1,724 today), second class $60 ($690 today), and third-class tickets were $30–$40 ($172–$460 today).

69. When the *Titanic* anchored in Queenstown, Ireland, to pick up passengers and mail, small boats followed the tender out to sea to sell articles of tweeds and lace to passengers. On one of these boats, Colonel John Jacob Astor bought an $800 lace shawl for his wife.

70. The *Titanic* carried 57,600 pieces of crockery, 29,000 pieces of glassware, and 44,000 pieces of cutlery, which were used by the passengers to dine with in the elegant dining saloons.

71. The last known picture taken of Captain E.J. Smith was snapped by Father Francis Browne when departing from the *Titanic* at Queenstown, Ireland. The photo shows Captain Smith peering down from the bridge of the *Titanic*.

72. The *Titanic* carried a 50-phone switchboard.

73. Seven stokers and firemen, otherwise known as the "black gang," were not included in the ship's crew after they arrived too late to board on the *Titanic's* maiden voyage.

74. Provisions on the *Titanic* included five tons of sugar and 1,221 quarts of oysters.

75. The first- and second-class kitchens, pantries, bakeries, and sculleries were located on D Deck between the first- and second-class dining saloons. The *Titanic* employed 300 in its kitchens.

76. A number of the original *Titanic* wireless messages, including one that stated "We have struck an iceberg," and other documents were sold at Christie's auction house in New York City Feb. 17, 1998, for more than 15 times their estimated value, a total of $180,310.

77. The main Promenade Deck on the *Titanic* was over 500 feet long while the Boat Deck was 200 feet in length.

78. The first-class dining saloon was 92 feet wide and 114 feet long and featured oak furniture with tables that could accommodate two, four, six, or eight people.

79. Each link of the *Titanic's* anchor chains weighed 175 pounds.

80. "When anyone asks me how I can best describe my experiences of nearly 40 years at sea, I merely say 'uneventful.' I have never been in an accident of any sort worth speaking about. I never saw a wreck and have never been wrecked, nor was I ever in any predicament that threatened to end in disaster of any sort."— Captain E.J. Smith's response to the New York press in 1907.

81. This passage was published in the magazine *The Shipbuilder* describing the first-class quarters on the *Titanic*: "The first-class public rooms include the dining saloon, reception room, restaurant, lounge, reading and writing room, smoking room, and the verandah cafes and palm courts. Other novel features are the gymnasium, squash racket court, Turkish and electric baths, and the swimming bath. Magnificent suites of rooms, and cabins of size and style sufficiently diverse to suit the likes and dislikes of any passenger, are provided. There is also a barber's shop, a dark room for photographers, a clothes-pressing room, a special dining room for maids and valets, a lending library, a telephone system, and a wireless telegraphy installation. Indeed, everything has been done in regard to the furniture and fittings to make the first-class accommodation more than equal to that provided in the finest hotels on the shore."

82. *Titanic* passengers had to pay $1 to take a Turkish bath.

83. An alternative to eating in the dining saloon on the *Titanic* was to eat at the Cafe Parisien, which was styled like sidewalk cafe in Paris, complete with wicker furniture and real French waiters.

84. *Titanic's* hull number at the Harland & Wolff shipyard in Belfast, Ireland, was 390904, a number many of the Catholic workers believed was a mirror image of the words "NO POPE."

85. The original name of *Titanic's* sister ship was *Gigantic*, but it was changed to a "luckier" name, the *Britannic*. The *Britannic* met the same fate as *Titanic* when she sunk in the Aegean Sea after being commissioned as a hospital ship and striking a mine in 1916 during World War I.

86. Construction began on *Titanic* on March 31, 1909, when the keel of the ship was laid in the shipyard of Harland & Wolff in Belfast, Ireland.

87. "It took me 14 days before I could find my way with confidence from one part of the ship to the other . . . a sailor does not walk about with a plan in his pocket, he must carry the ship in his head."—Second Officer Charles Lightoller describing the *Titanic's* immense size.

88. Some of the features of the gymnasium on the *Titanic* included rowing machines, stationary bicycles, a mechanical horse, and a mechanical camel.

89. The *Titanic* and the *Olympic* were the first ships to have swimming pools. The *Titanic* pool was located on E-deck and cost one shilling to use.

90. The *Titanic* carried 14 lifeboats, two emergency cutters, and four collapsible lifeboats, equaling 20 vessels that could accommodate 1,178 passengers and crew.

91. British painter Norman Wilkinson had two paintings adorning the interiors of the White Star Line's two sister ships, *Olympic* and *Titanic*, both of which were featured over the fireplaces in the first-class smoking rooms. The painting on the *Titanic* was titled "Plymouth Harbour"; the one on the *Olympic* was "Approach to the New World."

92. There were 13 honeymoon couples, including eight traveling first class. Among the first class newlyweds were Mr. and Mrs. John Jacob Astor, John and Nelle Snyder, and Daniel and Mary Marvin. Mrs. Astor and Mrs. Marvin lost their husbands when the *Titanic* sank.

93. The eight bandsmen boarded the *Titanic* at Southampton and were listed as second-class passengers on ticket number 250654.

94. The third-class Promenade Deck was located on the Shelter Deck or C Deck at the stern of the *Titanic*. Third-class passengers were not allowed access to the first- or second-class promenade areas. The first class, even though they had the largest promenade space, could move freely about the ship.

95. The Heart of the Ocean is the fabulous 56-carat diamond in the 1997 movie *Titanic*. The diamond necklace was given to Rose DeWitt Buckater by her fiance Caledon Hockley and closely resembles the famed Hope Diamond. In the spring of 1998 the Home Shopping Network sold copies of the Heart of the Ocean from the R.J. Graziano collection for $55.

96. Begun in 1958 by 18-year-old Edward Kamuda and other interested individuals, the *Titanic* Enthusiasts of America was established with 45 members. The group produces its own newsletter/journal, the *Titanic Communicator*, and is now known as the *Titanic* Historical Society with thousands of members worldwide.

97. The 1958 British movie *A Night To Remember*, a time capsule of the *Titanic* disaster, was described by *The New York Times* as "a tense, exciting, and supremely awesome drama." The film, which featured 200 speaking parts and cost $1,680,000 to make, starred David McCallum as junior wireless operator Harold Bride, Kenneth More as Second Officer Charles Lightoller and Honor Blackman. Sean Connery appeared in a minor role. In 1994 McCallum narrated the four-hour A&E documentary *Titanic: Death of a Dream/The Legend Lives On.*

98. Breakfast on *Titanic* was served from 8:30–10:30 a.m., lunch was served from 1–2:30 p.m., and dinner was served from 6–7:30 p.m. The a la carte restaurant served patrons between the hours of 8 a.m. and 11 p.m.

99. The *Titanic* employed six lookouts. Frederick Fleet and Reginald Lee were the two on watch in the crow's nest when *Titanic* struck the deadly iceberg.

100. A close personal friend of United States President William Howard Taft, Major Archibald Butt also served as a military aide to President Taft and died on the *Titanic*.

101. The 28-foot model of the *Titanic*, which was used during the filming of Twentieth Century Fox's 1953 *Titanic*, can be seen at the Marine Museum in Fall River, Massachusetts.

102. The *Californian* and *Carpathia*, enmeshed in the *Titanic* disaster, were both sunk by German U-boats, the *Californian* in 1917, and the *Carpathia* in 1918.

103. A 200-ton floating crane owned by Harland & Wolff was used to fit out the *Titanic*. The crane could lift 150 tons to a height of over 149 feet.

104. Frederick Wright was the pro squash supervisor on board the *Titanic*. It cost two shillings to use the squash court.

105. The *Titanic*, if she stood upright on her stern, would have been taller than any building in 1912.

106. The rudder of the *Titanic*, which enabled the ship to maneuver, was 78 feet 8 inches high with its six sections weighing 101 tons.

107. Among the passengers on the *Titanic* was Thomas Andrews, the director, chief draughtsman, and nephew of Lord Pirrie, chairman of Harland & Wolff, the builders of the *Titanic*. Andrews was on board the *Titanic* to inspect the structural aspects even down to the numbers of screws which were used in the hat racks. Andrews went down with his greatest creation.

108. Three ship's bells were on the *Titanic*. The first was 23 inches in diameter and could be found at the foot of the foremast. The second was 17 inches in diameter and was located in the crow's nest and was the bell that was rung by lookout Frederick Fleet to notify the bridge of the iceberg ahead. The third bell, nine inches in diameter, was on the bridge.

109. The maiden voyage of the *Titanic* lasted four days and 17 hours.

110. American financier J.P. Morgan, whose International Mercantile Marine controlled the White Star Line, canceled his booking on the *Titanic* due to illness.

111. Sixth Officer James P. Moody was one of the officers on duty at the moment *Titanic* struck an iceberg and he answered the phone call from the crow's nest that notified the bridge of the danger ahead.

112. The final song played by the *Titanic* orchestra on Sunday, April 14, 1912, during a church service led by Captain E.J. Smith, was *O God Our Help in Ages Past*.

113. The *Titanic* had three propellers. The center propeller measured 16 1/2 feet and had four blades. Each of the other propellers had a diameter of 23 1/2 feet and three blades.

114. The *Royal Mail Steamer Titanic* contained 29 three-story-high boilers, which served as the energy source that supplied the two triple-expansion engines and single turbine that drove the *Titanic*.

115. First-class passengers eating in the first-class dining saloon could drink "Draught Munich lager beer" for a sixpence a pint.

116. The *Titanic* had two barber shops on board, one in the first class and one in the second class. The barber shops also sold souvenirs, postcards and plates.

117. After being promoted to Commodore of the White Star Line in 1904, Edward J. Smith captained every flagship of the White Star Line until his death.

118. It took the greatest vessel ever built (at that time), a total of two hours and forty minutes to sink.

119. The crow's nest on the *Titanic* had a locker for binoculars, a telephone which was used to talk to the bridge, a bell which, if rung, alerted the bridge of danger ahead, and could accommodate two crewmen standing up.

120. The *Titanic's* board of trade number was 131,428.

121. Three professional card sharps were on board the *Titanic* under assumed names hoping to make some easy money on the new White Star Line ship. These men included George (Boy) Bradley, listed as "George Brayton," C.H. Romaine as "C. Rolmane," and Henry (Kid) Homer as "E. Haven."

122. The second grand staircase on the *Titanic* was located between the last two funnels and was not as elegant as the forward grand staircase but was still a prominent feature on the *Titanic*.

123. The china and glass used on the *Titanic* was supplied by J. Stonier and Company and had been put on board in Belfast prior to her sea trials.

124. The wireless cabin on the *Titanic* had three rooms. One was the sleeping quarters of the two wireless operators, Phillips and Bride, one was the actual wireless operating room, and the last was a dynamo room.

125. The *Titanic* was originally planned by Harland & Wolff to carry 48 lifeboats, but the number was reduced to 16 lifeboats and four collapsible lifeboats to give passengers more promenade space.

126. The *Titanic* had eight main decks, the top being the boat deck, that were labeled A, B, C, D, E, F, and G with the boat deck being A Deck. The boiler rooms and cargo holds were located below G Deck.

127. In 1886 and 1892, writer W.T. Stead, a casualty of the *Titanic*, wrote two separate short stories about ships colliding with the loss of many lives due to a shortage of lifeboats, much like that of the *Titanic*. Stead was last seen in the first-class smoking room reading alone.

128. Famed *Titanic* author Walter Lord was given the whistle belonging to Second Officer Charles Lightoller. This was the whistle Lightoller used to attract the other *Titanic* lifeboats to the overturned collapsible B. It has not been blown since that fateful night.

129. One of themost lavish areas on the *Titanic* was the first-class grand staircase, which was styled in late 17th-century William-and-Mary style with a contemporary Louis-14th balustrade that was paneled in oak and included a glass skylight. The grand staircase was located between the first two funnels.

130. In a romantic plot similar to the 1997 movie *Titanic*, Samuel Morley, who was already married, boarded the *Titanic* in 1912 with one of his employees, 19-year-old Kate Phillips, under the surname Mr. and Mrs. Marshall to start a new life in America. Phillips survived the *Titanic* disaster while Morley did not.

131. The wireless call letters for the *Titanic* were "MGY."

132. The reciprocating engines of the *Titanic* generated 15,000 horsepower at 75 revolutions per minute for the two outside propellers.

133. *Titanic* passenger Helen Bishop was accompanied by her dog Frou Frou, which stayed with her in her cabin during the voyage instead of the dog kennels. Frou Frou did not survive.

134. Captain Edward J. Smith had an illustrious career on the sea before going down with the *Titanic*. He commanded the *Republic, Coptic, Majestic, Baltic, Adriadic, Olympic*, and the ill-fated *Titanic*.

135. Shortly before the *Titanic's* voyage, survivor Colonel Archibald Gracie wrote a book titled *The Truth about Chickamauga*. While on the *Titanic*, Colonel Gracie had Macy's magnate Isidor Straus peruse the novel, which Straus replied he had read with "intense interest."

136. First Officer William Murdoch was in command of the *Titanic* when she struck the iceberg at 11:40 p.m., April 14, 1912. Quartermaster Robert Hitchens was at the ship's wheel with Quartermaster Alfred Oliver assisting. Also on the bridge were Fourth Officer Joseph Boxhall and Sixth Officer James Moody.

137. Since 1871, nearly every vessel owned by the White Star Line, owners of the *Titanic*, ended with the suffix "ic."

138. The *Titanic* had 150 separate electric motors to supply it with the electricity needed for the cranes, winches, watertight doors, telegraphs, telephones, and its Marconi wireless set.

139. The first-class dining saloon seated 532 diners; the second-class dining saloon seated 394; and the third-class dining saloon could seat 473.

140. From noon on Thursday, April 11, to noon on Friday, April 12, the *Titanic* covered 464 sea miles on its way to New York. From Friday, April 12, at noon to noon on Saturday, April 13, the *Titanic* sailed 519 sea miles.

141. *Titanic* lookout Frederick Lee was paid 5 pounds per month or about $25, plus five shillings extra lookout money per voyage.

142. Between April 12 and 14 the *Titanic* received eight ice warnings from the *Amerika, Baltic, Californian, Caronia, Mesaba,* and *Rappahannock* prior to its collision with the iceberg. Unfortunately, not all of these messages reached the bridge.

143. The *Titanic* was equipped to carry 905 people in first class, 564 in second class, 1,134 in third class, and 914 crew members, which totaled 3,547 people that the ship could accommodate.

144. There were a total of 159 furnaces, which supplied the *Titanic* with the power to reach speeds of at least 21 knots.

145. The *Titanic* and her sister ship the *Olympic* were photographed together on March 6, 1912, for the last time.

146. When he took the helm of the *Titanic*, Captain Edward J. Smith was the highest paid seaman operating a ship. His salary was 1,250 pounds a month, plus he could collect a non-collision bonus of 200 more pounds if his ship was not involved in an accident, making for a grand total of about $11,250 a year.

147. The lookouts on the *Titanic* might have spotted the danger in their path earlier if they had had binoculars. For reasons unknown the binoculars were not in the crow's nest but had been there during the ship's test run. Second Officer Lightoller confessed in later years that the binoculars were on the boat but were locked in a metal storage cabinet and nobody had a key.

148. The second-class passengers had two promenade areas on the *Titanic* with the largest one being 145 feet long, which was smaller than the smallest promenade area available to first-class passengers.

149. The *Carpathia*, the ship that rescued the survivors of the *Titanic*, was 58 miles to the southwest when it received the initial distress call.

150. On Sunday, April 14, the fateful day that the *Titanic* struck the iceberg, assistant purser Reginald Barker led the second class in a religious service.

151. F.G. Bealing and Son, a nursery and horticultural florist, supplied the White Star Line with between 300–400 plants in five-inch pots and the flowers that decorated the public rooms on the *Titanic*, including the first-class dining saloon, the ala carte restaurant, the Palm Court, and the Verandah Cafe.

152. The *Titanic* was a mere two miles short of the *Olympic's* record for the best run in a day after covering 546 miles between noon on Saturday, April 13, to noon on Sunday, April 14.

153. The 28 new staterooms on the *Titanic*, which were not found on the *Titanic's* sister ship the *Olympic*, were located on B Deck and had real windows instead of the usual portholes.

154. The third-class dining saloon was located amidships on F Deck. The walls in the dining saloon were painted in white enamel and were decorated with framed White Star posters.

155. Captain E.J. Smith and his six officers were housed on the forward boat deck directly behind the wheelhouse of the *Titanic*.

156. The *Titanic* was built with a companionway on E Deck that stretched from one end of the ship to the other and was known to the officers as the "Park Lane," while the crew called the corridor "Scotland Road."

157. Although it has never been proven, it appears that a well-known gambler named Jay Yates, who also used the alias J.H. Rogers, was on board the *Titanic* despite the fact that neither of these names ever appear in the passenger lists. Apparently, Yates gave a farewell note signed "Rogers" to a survivor, which leads many to believe that this card sharp lost his life when the ship sank.

158. The middle propeller on the *Titanic* was powered by a low-pressure turbine that generated 16,000 horsepower at 165 revolutions per minute.

159. "An iceberg sir. I hard-a-starboarded and reversed the engines and I was going to hard-a-port around it, but she was too close. I could not do any more."—First Officer William Murdoch's reply to Captain Smith as the Captain rushed onto the bridge after the *Titanic* collided with the iceberg.

160. Senior Wireless Operator Jack Phillips sent the *Titanic's* first distress call at 12:15 a.m.

161. Paneled in mahogany and featuring a real fireplace, the *Titanic's* smoking room on the Promenade Deck was a favorite of the gentlemen after dinner.

162. The last position of *Titanic*, which was charted by Fourth Officer Joseph Groves Boxhall and transmitted by Senior Wireless Operator John Phillips, was 41°46'N, 50°14'W.

163. Many of the first-class staterooms, some of the most elegant found in the ships of 1912, were styled in Louis 14th, Louis 15th, Louis 16th, Empire, Italian Renaissance, Georgian, Regance, Queen Anne, and Modern and Old Dutch.

164. Wealthy first-class passenger John Jacob Astor and his 19-year-old wife Madeleine were accompanied on *Titanic* by their Airdale Kitty. Astor, 48, reportedly the richest person on board, and his pregnant wife occupied stateroom C62, the parlour suite on C deck.

165. During the filming of *Titanic* (1997), which wound up with 6,029 stunt person days (the equivalent of one stuntman doing stunts all day, every day, seven days a week for 16 years), only three injuries occurred. Two construction workers were reported killed while building the original ship in Belfast, Ireland.

166. The post office on the *Titanic* took up two deck levels and carried 3,435 bags of mail and 900 tons of baggage. There were five postal clerks: three American, William Logan Gwinn, Oscar S. Woody, and John Starr March; and two British, John Richard Jago Smith and James Bertram Williamson. They were the first victims.

167. On April 14, 1912, the night *Titanic* struck the iceberg, Captain Edward J. Smith joined the Carters, Thayers, and Major Archibald Butt in attending a dinner party in the a la carte restaurant that was given by Mr. and Mrs. George D. Widener.

168. When Captain Smith asked designer Thomas Andrews for an estimate of how much time they had after the designer made an inspection of the damage from the iceberg, Andrews replied, "I give her an hour, maybe two, not much more."

169. The *Titanic* had two sister ships, the *Olympic* which was built before *Titanic*, and the *Britannic* which was built after *Titanic*.

170. NBC paid $30 million for the rights to air the 1997 film *Titanic* for five runs, beginning in the year 2000.

171. The speed of the *Titanic* when it struck the iceberg was 21–22 knots or about 26–27 miles per hour.

172. Actress Dorothy Gibson, a *Titanic* survivor, co-wrote and starred in the silent movie *Saved From the Titanic* on May 14, 1912, just one month after the *Titanic* sank. She wore the same dress in the film that she was wearing the night of the disaster.

173. It is now believed that the *Titanic* sailed for a full 20 minutes after colliding with the iceberg before it came to a complete halt.

174. "We're dressed in our best and are prepared to go down like gentlemen." —Benjamin Guggenheim after he and his valet Victor Giglio returned to their staterooms and reappeared on deck in evening clothes, prepared for the inevitable.

175. No one is sure of what the final song was played by the band aboard *Titanic*. Many believe the tune was *Nearer My God to Thee* but stronger evidence points to *Songe d'Automne*.

176. *Titanic's* 14 Academy Award nominations tied the 1997 film for the most ever, with 1950's *All About Eve*.

177. Twenty-one-year-old Harold Thomas Cottam was the sole wireless operator on the *Carpathia* and one of those directly responsible for saving the 705 survivors of *Titanic*.

178. "She's gone; that's the last of her."—Said by a survivor in lifeboat #13 after the *Titanic* sank.

179. Fourth Officer Boxhall attempted to reach the "mystery ship" seen by many of the officers and passengers on the *Titanic* by Morse lamp but never made contact.

180. Douglas Spedden, a 7-year-old *Titanic* passenger, brought along a white stuffed bear named Polar. This bear escaped in lifeboat #3 with the lad.

181. Daisy Spedden wrote *Polar the Titanic* Bear about the *Titanic* story as seen through the eyes of her son's stuffed bear as a gift for her son in 1913. Published in 1994, the book has sold over 250,000 copies.

182. It took two lifebelts to cover Dr. Hugo Frauenthal, who weighed close to 300 pounds.

183. The band of the *Titanic* consisted of bandleader/violinist Wallace Hartley, violinist C. Krims, cellist R. Bricoux, pianist W.T. Brailey, pianist P.C. Taylor, cellist J.W. Woodward, bass player J.F.C. Clarke, and violinist J.L. Hume.

184. The 14 regular lifeboats on the *Titanic* could accommodate 65 people. The two emergency boats (#s 1 and 2) could accommodate 40 people. The four collapsible lifeboats, A, B, C, and D, could each accommodate 47 passengers and crew.

185. No one woke Fifth Officer Harold Lowe to inform him of the danger that had transpired on the *Titanic*. Instead, he heard noises outside his cabin and looked out the porthole to see people in lifebelts. He immediately got dressed and began assisting passengers into the lifeboats.

186. Stewart Collet, a Second Officer survivor of the *Titanic*, took his Bible with him off the ship because of a promise he had made to his brother that he would take it everywhere with him until they met again.

187. At 12:45 a.m. on April 15, 1912, Fourth Officer Joseph G. Boxhall fired the first distress rocket, which was reportedly seen by officers and crew of the *Californian*.

188. American Frank Carlson was on his way to Cherbourg, France, to board the *Titanic*, when, fortunately, his car broke down and he missed the ship. However, he was still listed on the passenger manifesto and also as a casualty of the disaster.

189. The temperature of the Atlantic the night the *Titanic* sank was 28 degrees.

190. Among the newspaper errors in reporting the sea calamity, the *St. Petersburg Times* front-page headline of April 16, 1912, misspelled the name of the ship the *Titanic* as the "Titantic"; but the *New York Evening Sun's* afternoon edition of April 15 reported: "All Saved From Titanic After Collision."

191. The debut episode of Irwin Allen's 1965 sci-fi TV series *The Time Tunnel* features co-stars James Darren and Robert Colbert as scientists attempting to change history as they go back in time to the *Titanic*.

192. While loading lifeboat #14, Fifth Officer Harold Lowe fired his gun three times along the side of the ship to discourage any attempts by the passengers on deck to jump into the lifeboat.

193. Going down with the *Titanic* was a jewel-encrusted, priceless copy of *The Rubaiyat*.

194. Being the first lifeboat lowered on the port side at 12:55 a.m, lifeboat #6 included Major Peuchen, Molly Brown, lookout Frederick Fleet and was commanded by Quartermaster Robert Hitchens. The boat carried 28 people, 37 less than what the boat could accommodate.

195. The 1997 *Titanic* film featured a fictional character named Jack Dawson, while a real-life victim of the disaster, buried in Fairview Cemetery in Halifax, Nova Scotia, was named James Dawson.

196. At 12:45 a.m. lifeboat #7 was the first lifeboat lowered from the starboard side of the *Titanic*. It carried 28 people, including actress Dorothy Gibson.

197. Legend holds that one man dressed as a woman to secure a lifeboat seat, but it was actually a man who pulled a woman's shawl over his head.

198. Lady Bellamy from the highly-acclaimed British TV drama *Upstairs, Downstairs* (1973) meets her demise on the *Titanic*.

199. Helen Churchill Candee gave Edward A. Kent an ivory and gold miniature of her mother before she climbed into a lifeboat. The keepsake was returned to her after Kent's body was recovered from the Atlantic and the miniature was found in his jacket pocket.

200. Before going to the boat deck moments before the *Titanic* sank, Major Archibald Butt, Arthur Ryerson, Frank Millet, and Clarence Moore were all seen in the first-class smoking room at 2 a.m. playing one last hand of cards.

201. The *Titanic's* 75-year record for the worst peace-time sea-disaster was shattered in 1987 when a ferry in the Philippines sank, killing 4,375 people.

202. The two embossed name-plates on the stern section of the *Titanic*, reading "*Titanic*" and "Liverpool," were 18 inches high.

203. Not one of the 34 engineering officers serving on the *Titanic* survived. Their heroics were the only reason that the *Titanic* had electricity for the wireless unit and that the lights continued to burn until the final moments of the *Titanic's* life, 2:18 a.m., just two minutes before the *Titanic* plunged to the bottom of the Atlantic.

204. Of the officers on the *Titanic*, only four survived the sinking: Second Officer Charles Lightoller, Third Officer Herbert Pitman, Fourth Officer Joseph Boxhall, and Fifth Officer Harold Lowe. Boxhall assisted in production of the 1958 film *A Night To Remember.*

205. Of the two dogs that survived the *Titanic*, one was a Pomeranian belonging to Margaret Hays that accompanied her in lifeboat #7, while the other was Sun Yat-sen, a Pekinese belonging to Henry Sleeper Harper, that found refuge in lifeboat #3 with his owner.

206. The musical *The Unsinkable Molly Brown*, based on the story of Molly Brown, premiered on Broadway in 1960. In 1964 the play was transformed into a movie starring Debbie Reynolds as Brown.

207. The *Titanic* Historical Society, based in Indian Orchard, Massachusetts, owns a variety of *Titanic* memorabilia, including a razor that belonged to a steward, a ship's menu, lookout Frederick Fleet's discharge book, and the lifebelt worn by Madeleine Astor.

208. Lifeboat #3 left the *Titanic* at 1 a.m. with 40 people on board, including 15 crew members.

209. Filled with five people over the lifeboat's maximum capacity, lifeboat #15 left the *Titanic* with 70 people, including 13 crew members.

210. Jack Dawson, the American drifter and love interest of Rose DeWitt Buckater in the 1997 movie *Titanic*, who luckily wins a third-class ticket aboard *Titanic* through a game of poker, was played by romeo Leonardo DiCaprio. The actor received $2.5 million for his work.

211. Written by Peter Stone with music by Maury Yeston, the Broadway musical *Titanic* won five Tony awards in 1997, including Best Musical. The play's finale features a sloping stage.

212. "Men, you have done your full duty. You can do no more. Abandon your cabin. Now it's every man for himself."—Captain Edward J. Smith.

213. As Jack Phillips sweated over the wireless moments before the *Titanic* sank, Harold Bride encountered a stoker who was trying to steal Phillips' lifebelt. A scuffle ensued and the last time the two wireless officers saw the stoker, he was lying unconscious on the floor of the wireless cabin, a casualty of their actions.

214. "I must be a gentleman."—Walter D. Douglas to his wife as she was getting into a lifeboat. Douglas perished on the *Titanic* along with many other men who decided to follow through with the time-honored tradition that women and children should be loaded into lifeboats before men.

215. The Countess of Rothes manned the tiller of lifeboat #8 after leaving the *Titanic* at 1:10 a.m. with notable passengers such as French aviator Pierre Marechal and sculptor Paul Chevre.

216. Stewardess Violet Jessop, who also survived the sinking of the *Titanic's* sister ship, the *Britannic*, was one of the 56 people that left the *Titanic* aboard lifeboat #16. She wrote her memoirs in the book *Titanic Survivor*.

217. The prop necklace used in the 1997 film *Titanic* was not a real diamond but made of cubic zirconium gold.

218. Asprey Jewelers of England have made a replica of the Heart of the Ocean, the necklace in the 1997 movie *Titanic*. The necklace cost around $3.5 million and was made from a 165-carat Ceylon sapphire.

219. Grouped in fours with 190 feet separating the two groups, there were eight lifeboats on both the port and starboard sides of the *Titanic* with four Englehardt collapsible canvas lifeboats stored on the officers' rooftop.

220. Lifeboat #1 left the *Titanic* at 1:10 a.m. with only 12 people on board a lifeboat that accommodated 40. Lifeboat #2 was lowered from the decks of the *Titanic* at 1:45 a.m. with a capacity of 40 and only 25 people on board.

221. Major Arthur Peuchen, vice-commodore of the Royal Canadian Yacht Club, was the only male passenger Second Officer Charles Lightoller let into lifeboat #6 after learning that Peuchen was a yachtsman and that lifeboat #6 was in desperate need of an experienced seaman.

222. Collapsible C was launched from the *Titanic* at 1:40 a.m. with 42 people, including White Star Line Chairman J. Bruce Ismay. Collapsible C was the last boat lowered on the starboard side and was picked up by the *Carpathia* at 6:15 a.m.

223. Bernard Fox, who played Colonel Archibald Gracie in *Titanic* in 1997, was also in the 1958 film *A Night To Remember* in an unbilled role as lookout Frederick Fleet.

224. The lifeboats on the port side of the *Titanic* were even numbered while those on the starboard side were odd numbered.

225. One of the *Titanic* crewmen was the inspiration behind a teleplay that was titled *Lone Survivor*, which later paved the way for Rod Serling's *The Twilight Zone*.

226. First-class passenger Benjamin Guggenheim was worth a reported $100 million when he died, or more than $4 billion in today's dollars.

227. "You fellows need not to worry about that. I will give you a fiver each to start a new kit."—Sir Cosmo Duff Gordon to the crew members of the *Titanic* who were in lifeboat #1 with him. Gordon paid each crewman in the boat five pounds to help buy a new kit which they lost when the *Titanic* sank.

228. The *Titanic* sent two distress calls. The first was "C.Q.D." (Come Quick, Danger), which was adopted in 1904 and was the Morse distress call used during the first years of wireless telegraphy. SOS was adopted at the Berlin Convention in 1908, and was becoming the prevalent wireless code for distress. The wireless officers on the *Titanic* originally began to use the CQD distress call but then began using the SOS.

229. After almost having lifeboat #15 lowered on top of it, lifeboat #13 rowed away from the *Titanic* at 1:25 a.m. with 64 people.

230. At 1:55 a.m., lifeboat #4 left the *Titanic* with 45 people on board, including Madeleine Astor, Mrs. Arthur Ryerson, Mrs. John B. Thayer, and Mrs. George D. Widener.

231. Despite shooting the majority of the 1997 movie *Titanic* in Rosarita, Mexico, and filming various sequences of the actual wreck of the *Titanic* for use in the movie, director James Cameron also shot various scenes in Halifax, Nova Scotia, the place where 150 unclaimed victims of the *Titanic* disaster were laid to rest.

232. Collapsible A was never launched but floated off the ship half swamped with Rosa Abbott and 12 men.

233. David Warner, who played Spicer Lovejoy in 1997's *Titanic*, was also in the 1979 TV movie *S.O.S. Titanic*, as Lawrence Beesley. This was the first *Titanic* movie to use special effects and create a computer-generated *Titanic*.

234. Tennis star Norris Williams pedaled a stationary bike in the gymnasium to pass the time as the *Titanic* sank. Karl H. Behr, a first-class survivor of the *Titanic*, was a member of the American Davis Cup tennis team.

235. After his wife was put into lifeboat #5, Dr. Hugo W. Frauenthal jumped into the boat as it was being lowered, landing on Annie Stengel and breaking two of her ribs and knocking her unconscious.

236. The *Titanic's* boat deck, from where the lifeboats were launched the night of April 14–15, and the *Titanic's* bridge were 70 feet above the waterline.

237. One of the three messages J. Bruce Ismay sent to the White Star Line's New York office was to American International Mercantile Marine Vice-President Philip A.S. Franklin. It stated: "Deeply regret advise you *Titanic* sank this morning after collision with iceberg, resulting in serious loss of life. Full particulars later."

238. The *Titanic* fired eight white distress rockets that were observed by *Californian* apprentice James Gibson. This lends support to the theory that the *Californian* was in a position to save many of the lives lost on the *Titanic*.

239. The last time anyone saw Thomas Andrews, managing director of Harland & Wolff and a passenger who was on the *Titanic* to oversee her voyage, he was staring into space in front of the fireplace in the first-class smoking room.

240. The *Titanic* was the second vessel belonging to the White Star Line that hit an iceberg and the second owned by the line that constituted the world's worst peacetime shipwreck.

241. Captain Arthur Rostron of the *Carpathia,* the savior of the *Titanic* survivors, made 240 pounds a year, 1,100 pounds less than *Titanic's* Captain Smith.

242. *Titanic* survivor Edith Russell carried a musical toy pig that played the song *Maxine* when its tail was pulled. She later gave the toy to *A Night To Remember* author Walter Lord.

243. Chief Wireless Operator Jack Phillips reportedly reached the overturned collapsible B but died before the *Carpathia* arrived to rescue the *Titanic's* survivors.

244. Skeptics believe that if the *Titanic* had hit the iceberg head-on, she would not have sunk and would have lost only a few hundred passengers and crew. And experts have calculated that if all 16 compartments had been opened, the ship would have sunk on a more even keel, which would have given the *Carpathia* ample time to rescue more survivors.

245. *Titanic* was built in Belfast, Ireland, and almost 84 years later, *Titanic's* twin was built to 90% of her original size in Rosarito in Baja California, Mexico, for the filming of the 1997 movie *Titanic*. The replica was 775 feet long and 99 feet tall and rested in a 17-million gallon water tank.

246. Lifeboat #11 was lowered from the decks of the *Titanic* at 1:25 a.m. with 70 people on board, five more than the maximum capacity.

247. "It's all right, little girl, you go and I'll stay awhile."—Don Marvin as he blew a kiss to his new wife as she was being lowered into a lifeboat.

248. While sitting in the *Titanic's* gymnasium on one of the mechanical horses hours before the *Titanic* sank, John Jacob Astor took out his penknife and cut open a lifebelt he had in his lap to show his wife what was inside.

249. "I've always stayed with my husband; so why should I leave him now? We have been together for many years. Where you go, I go."—One of the most famous remarks made during the sinking of the *Titanic* by Ida Straus, wife of Macy's founder Isidor Straus, after she refused to get in lifeboat #8. The last time witnesses saw the couple, they were sitting on a pair of deck chairs.

250. After the *Titanic* sank, 14 people were rescued from the water, and only seven of those survived, including Rosa Abbott, the lone woman pulled from the Atlantic.

251. Col. Archibald Gracie ran into the *Titanic's* squash pro Fred Wright at 12:30 a.m., just two short hours before the *Titanic* sank. Gracie joked around with Wright saying, "Hadn't we better cancel that appointment?" Gracie had reserved the court for 7:30 the next morning.

252. Lifeboat 14 was the only one that returned to rescue victims from the icy waters of the *Titanic* site.

253. Twenty-one-year-old David Sarnoff, who had a wireless shack on top of a skyscraper in New York, intercepted the first news of the *Titanic* disaster on April 15.

254. "We are safer here than in that little boat."—John Jacob Astor's response to the *Titanic's* officers' request that the lifeboats should be loaded.

255. "As row by row of the porthole lights of the *Titanic* sank into the sea, this was about all one could see. When the *Titanic* upended to sink, all was blacked out until the tons of machinery crashed to the bow. This sounded like an explosion, which of course it was not. As this happened the hundreds and hundreds of people were thrown into the sea. It isn't likely I shall ever forget the screams of these people as they perished in water said to be 28 degrees."—*Titanic* survivor Marshall Drew.

256. The men that survived the *Titanic* disaster on the overturned collapsible B were picked up by lifeboat #12 and then taken aboard the *Carpathia*.

257. The last lifeboat to leave the *Titanic*, collapsible D, was lowered at 2:05 a.m. April 15, 1912.

258. When the iceberg, which stuck about 100 feet above the water, sideswiped the *Titanic*, it shoved chunks of ice through the open porthole of passenger James B. McGough and they fell to his cabin floor.

259. Close to 30 men clung to the overturned collapsible B, including Second Officer Charles Lightoller, Junior Wireless Operator Harold Bride, Colonel Archibald Gracie, and Chief Baker Charles Joughin.

260. Second Officer Charles Lightoller refused a seat in collapsible D at 2:05 a.m., a mere 15 minutes before the *Titanic* sank, to go down with the ship. Later he was able to climb aboard the overturned collapsible B. The *Titanic's* highest-ranking surviving officer, he was the last survivor to board the *Carpathia*.

261. The only person to return to the wreckage of the *Titanic* to pick up any possible survivors was Fifth Officer Harold Lowe, who corralled lifeboats 10, 12, 4, and collapsible D together with his own lifeboat 14, and then distributed the passengers in number 14 to the other boats, and returned to the wreckage with a handpicked crew in hopes of saving others.

262. The bow section of the *Titanic* lies in the Atlantic Ocean at 41°43'57" N, 49°56'49" W. The separated stern section of the *Titanic* lies at 41°43'35" N, 49°56'54" W.

263. The final distress rocket from the *Titanic* was fired at 1:40 a.m.

264. The pay of the crew on the *Titanic* ceased when the *Titanic* sank at 2:20 a.m. April 15, 1912.

265. After rescuing the few survivors on it, Fifth Officer Harold Lowe set collapsible A afloat on the open sea with three bodies in it. On May 13, 1912, almost a month after the disaster, the White Star Line's *Oceanic* found collapsible A drifting 230 miles from the last reported position of the sinking.

266. The *Carpathia* rescued 705 *Titanic* survivors.

267. On the menu for the final meal those in third class enjoyed was vegetable soup, roasted pork with sage and pearl onions (or fresh fish), green peas, boiled potatoes, plum pudding with a sweet sauce, cookies, a variety of cheeses, and fresh oranges.

268. After befriending one another on the *Carpathia*, Robert Daniel and Mary Eloise Smith (Smith's husband Lucien was one of the casualties of the *Titanic* disaster) were married two years later.

269. The *Titanic* did not radio for help until 35 minutes after the collision with the iceberg.

270. Commanded by Fourth Officer Joseph Boxhall, lifeboat #2 was the only one with signal flares. The green flares aided the crew of the *Carpathia* in spotting the *Titanic's* lifeboats.

271. The International Mercantile Marine received this message after the disaster: "Inexpressible sorrow. Am proceeding straight on voyage. Carpathia informs me no hope in searching. Will send names survivors as obtainable. Yamsi." The name "Yamsi" was a code name used by J. Bruce Ismay, which spelled his name backwards.

272. Experts have estimated that the *Titanic* hit the ocean bottom at approximately 25–30 miles per hour.

273. At 4:10 a.m. on April 15, lifeboat #2, commanded by Fourth Officer Joseph Boxhall, became the first lifeboat to be picked up by the *Carpathia.* At 8:10 a.m. lifeboat #12 was the last to be lifted from the Atlantic.

274. The *Carpathia* docked at Pier 54 in New York at 9:25 p.m. on April 18, 1912, with the survivors of the *Titanic.*

275. In a twist of irony, Mr. and Mrs. Charles Marshall, passengers on the *Carpathia,* were awakened on the morning of the rescue by a steward who reported that their niece, Mrs. E.D. Appleton, would like to see them. It turned out that Mrs. Appleton and two other nieces were on board the *Titanic* and as each of them safely reached the *Carpathia's* decks, a family reunion was held.

276. *Titanic* passenger George Widener was worth $50 million at the time of his death, more than $2 billion in today's dollars.

277. When the *Titanic* was discovered, Dr. Robert Ballard was in his cabin reading Chuck Yeager's autobiography.

278. Five thousand, eight hundred and ninety-two tons of coal were loaded aboard the *Titanic* for her maiden voyage. The *Titanic* burned 690 tons of coal per day in 29 boilers. You can buy a lump of coal brought from the depths of the *Titanic* for $25, plus $4.95 shipping and handling. Call 1-800-600-3227. After the 1997 film debuted, orders went from five lumps per week to 150 per day.

279. All of the children in first class and second class were saved except one, Lorraine Allison.

280. Charles Wilson carved the central portion of the "Honour and Glory Crowning Time" panels that were featured in the first-class grand staircase on the *Olympic* and *Titanic*.

281. The portrait of Rose DeWitt Buckater that Jack Dawson sketched in the 1997 movie *Titanic* and which set the base as to their shipboard romance when researchers recover the safe in which the drawing was left, was drawn by director James Cameron.

282. "God himself could not sink this ship."—said by a deck hand to second-class passenger Mrs. Albert Caldwell when she asked if the *Titanic* was really unsinkable.

283. Harold Sidney Bride, the 22-year-old Junior Wireless Operator who survived the sinking of the *Titanic*, was paid a salary of a little less than $12 a month.

284. Michel and Edmond Navratil were kidnapped by their father Michel Navratil, who was listed on *Titanic's* passenger lists as Michel "Hoffman." Navratil perished on the *Titanic* while his sons escaped on the last lifeboat and were safely returned to their mother after being dubbed "the unknown orphans" of the *Titanic*.

285. First-class passenger Charlotte Drake Cardeza filed a 14-page, $177,352.75 claim against the White Star Line for loss of property including 14 trunks, four suitcases, three crates of baggage, 70 dresses, 10 fur coats, 38 large feather pieces, 22 hatpins, 91 pairs of gloves, and a Swiss musical box shaped like a bird.

286. The lifeboat scenes in the movie *A Night To Remember* were shot at Ruislip reservoir near Pinewood Studios. The ship seen slipping into the water in the beginning of the film is the *Queen Mary*.

287. In the cargo hold of the *Titanic* was William Carter's 25-horsepower Renault. Carter filed a $5,000 claim against the White Star Line for loss of property after losing the automobile, similar to one featured in the 1997 movie *Titanic*. Carter also lost 60 shirts, 15 pairs of shoes, two sets of tails, and 24 polo sticks.

288. The great sea disaster has inspired a $50 computer game *Titanic: Adventure Out of Time*, a two-disc CD-Rom, which allows players to tour the ship and participate in a spy game.

289. As of April 1, 1998, there were six survivors of the *Titanic* tragedy.

290. Madeleine Astor, pregnant when *Titanic* sank, gave birth to a son in August 1912, naming him after his deceased father, John Jacob Astor.

291. Robert W. Daniel filed a $750 loss of property claim against the White Star Line after losing his champion French bulldog Gamin de Pycombe on the *Titanic*.

292. A deckchair recovered after the *Titanic* sank is now on display at the Maritime Museum of the Atlantic in Halifax, Nova Scotia.

293. The 1992 novel *No Greater Love*, written by romance queen Danielle Steele, begins with the *Titanic's* fateful night.

294. One of the mysteries of the *Titanic* came to light in 1962 when a report made by Hendrik Naess became public. Naess, First Officer on board the Norwegian vessel *Samson,* claimed that the *Samson* had seen the *Titanic* and her distress rockets but failed to respond due to their illegal hunting of seals off southeastern Canada.

295. American postal clerk Oscar Scott Woody, who perished on the *Titanic*, died on his birthday, April 15, at the age of 44.

296. Clive Cussler's 1977 fictional bestseller *Raise the Titanic!* featured hero Dirk Pitt as part of an American Naval Expedition that brings the *Titanic* to the surface.

297. On July 17, 1980, Texas oilman Jack Grimm, who sponsored expeditions to search for Noah's ark, the Loch Ness monster, and Big Foot, sponsored several expeditions to search for the *Titanic*. All proved unsuccessful despite Grimm's persistent notion that his group had located one of the ship's propellers.

298. The 1991 film *Titanica* shows incredible images and haunting pictures of the *Titanic* at the bottom of the Atlantic, including a pair of empty stoker boots.

299. The only visible sign that remains of the *Titanic's* bridge today is the bronze telemeter that held the ship's wheel.

300. Seaman Jones mounted the number "8" from lifeboat number 8 and presented the plaque to the Countess of Rothes in recognition for her assistance in handling the tiller in the lifeboat that fateful night.

301. James and Mabel Fenwick, on the *Carpathia* bound for a Mediterranean honeymoon, took many photographs documenting the *Carpathia's* rescue of the *Titanic* survivors, including pictures of the lifeboats approaching the *Carpathia*.

302. President Taft commissioned the light cruiser *USS Chester* to help relay the *Carpathia's* messages and to inquire about his friend and Archibald Butt.

303. Arthur and Emily Ryerson and three of their children took the *Titanic* to America to bury a son who had been killed in an automobile accident in Pennsylvania. Mr. Ryerson died in the *Titanic* tragedy, and upon arrival in New York, Mrs. Ryerson attended funeral services for her husband and son.

304. The fate of the 13 lifeboats brought to New York by the *Carpathia,* the only relics left of the "unsinkable" *Titanic*, remains a mystery. After being dropped off at the White Star pier, the lifeboat company flags and nameplates were immediately removed by workers.

305. *Titanic* survivor Helen Churchill Candee wrote several books, including *How Women May Earn a Living, An Oklahoma Romance,* and *Decorative Styles and Periods,* a history of tapestry.

306. The White Star Line contracted the vessel *Mackay-Bennett* to recover the bodies from the Atlantic. The *Mackay-Bennett* retrieved 306, 116 of which were buried at sea while the other 190 bodies were taken to Halifax to be identified and buried.

307. The ships reported by the American inquiry to be close to the *Titanic* were the *Baltic, Birma, Californian,* the rescue ship *Carpathia, Frankfurt, Mount Temple,* the *Titanic's* sister ship *Olympic,* and the *Virginian.* The closest ship, according to the inquiry, was the *Californian* at 19 1/2 miles away, with the farthest being the *Olympic,* 512 miles away. This does not include several "mystery ships" reportedly in the area.

308. *Titanic* survivor Edith Rosenaum filed a claim for losses that included a $2 hot water bottle and $20 for property, powder, and rouge.

309. Led by Reverend Carter, nearly 100 passengers gathered in the second-class dining saloon on the evening of Sunday, April 14, the night the *Titanic* struck the iceberg. Douglas Norman played the piano while Marion Wright sang a solo, *Lead Kindly Light*, which Reverend Carter explained had been written after a ship sank on the Atlantic.

310. The Carpathia, the rescue ship of the survivors, was less than one-third the size of the *Titanic*.

311. Harold Bride, the surviving officer of the two that worked the wireless on the *Titanic*, worked for the Marconi Company for a while, then mysteriously disappeared around 1922. Bride reportedly died of bronchial carcinoma on April 29, 1956.

312. None of the third-class survivors of the *Titanic* were called to testify during the American Senate inquiry.

313. After 73 years at the bottom of the ocean, the *Titanic* was discovered at 1:05 a.m., Sept. 1, 1985, when Argo, the underwater eyes of the researchers, passed over a piece of man-made debris that was later identified as one of the *Titanic's* massive boilers.

314. The majority of crew members that signed up to work on the *Titanic* lived in Southampton, England. That town lost 549 men when the ship sank, leaving 232 widows and 1,239 children fatherless.

315. After the death of John Jacob Astor, his widow Madeleine received $1.7 million dollars in his will, while their unborn son was given a $3 million-dollar trust fund with an extra $5 million dollar inheritance when he came of age. After three marriages, Madeleine Astor committed suicide in 1937.

316. There are over 90 *Titanic* web sites on the Internet.

317. "MV Scotia, New York to Southampton, June 12, 1967, at 0938, Lat 41°46'N, Long 50°14'W, the cremated remains of the late commander J.G. Boxhall were scattered on the sea during a brief ceremony."—Taken from the log of the Cunard vessel *Scotia,* former *Titanic* Fourth Officer Boxhall's remains were scattered over the last reported position of the *Titanic*, the position that he himself charted.

318. The J. Peterman Company and 20th Century Fox sold props, costumes and other items from the 1997 film *Titanic*. A 13-foot fiberglass reproduction of the anchor from the ship and a 28-foot-long lifeboat, "not seaworthy," both used in the movie were listed for $25,000, while a canvas life jacket was priced at $95.

319. No officer that survived the *Titanic* disaster received their own command of a ship.

320. Hokan Bjornstrom-Steffanson, a first-class passenger on *Titanic*, filed a $100,000 claim for loss of property for a 4 x 8 feet oil painting by Blondel entitled "La Circasienne Au Bain."

321. The *Titanic* tragedy inspired many folk songs, including The *Titanic by Pop* Stoneman in 1915, as well as *Down With the Old Canoe, God Moves Over the Water, The Titanic (Cold and Icy Sea), The Titanic (Gone to Rest), The Titanic (Husbands and Wives), Titanic (Rise No More)*, and *The Titanic 6*.

322. In the 1989 movie *Ghostbusters II*, *Titanic* finally completes her maiden voyage to New York in the form of a ghost ship.

323. "The *Titanic* is a subject no one will ever tire of." —1997 *Titanic* executive producer Rae Sanchini.

324. After peddling newspapers on the streets of Southampton during his latter years, the man responsible for spotting the iceberg that sank the *Titanic*, lookout Frederick Fleet, committed suicide on January 10, 1965, at the age of 76.

325. The stern section of the *Titanic* lies 1,970 feet away from the bow section. Thanks to the discovery of the *Titanic* in 1985, the debate over whether the *Titanic* snapped in half as she sank was solved. The *Titanic* did break into two pieces at the surface before she sank.

326. In August 1996 R.M.S. *Titanic*, a company with exclusive rights to salvage anything from the *Titanic*, attempted to raise a 15-ton portion of the hull but lost the piece after the cables bringing it to the surface snapped. Witnesses included 1,700 paying tourists.

327. After gaining fame due to her behavior in lifeboat #6, the Denver socialite "The Unsinkable Molly Brown" died in 1932 at the age of 65 of a stroke. She lost a necklace worth $325,000 and 13 pairs of shoes on the *Titanic*.

328. The U.S. Congress recognized *Carpathia* Captain Arthur Rostron's efforts to save the survivors of the *Titanic* by awarding him a special gold medal.

329. Despite frostbitten feet, junior wireless officer Harold Bride assisted *Carpathia* wireless officer Harold Cottam in transmitting messages of the calamity to the world.

330. After boarding the *Carpathia,* J. Bruce Ismay, chairman of the White Star Line, confined himself to Dr. Frank McGee's cabin and did not come out again until the ship reached New York.

331. *New York Times* editor Carr Van Anda received a message just one hour after the sinking that verified the disaster.

332. The first-class *Titanic* survivors raised $4,360 among themselves, and the total eventually reached $15,000, for Captain Rostron and the crew of the *Carpathia* for their rescue efforts. The survivors also bought a silver cup for Rostron and 320 medals for the crew; gold medals for the senior officers, silver medals for the junior officers, and bronze medals for the rest of the crew.

333. After the survivors boarded the *Carpathia,* Father Roger Anderson, a passenger on the boat, led a service for the souls lost at sea. *Titanic* survivors and *Carpathia* passengers attended the service in the first-class dining salon.

334. Thomas Ryan sued the White Star Line for the loss of his son, third-class passenger Patrick Ryan, and received 100 pounds for his son's life or about $500.

335. Lost on the *Titanic* were four roosters and hens belonging to Ella Holmes White, for which she filed a claim for $207.87.

336. The movie soundtrack from the 1997 film *Titanic* is the fastest-selling and best-selling movie soundtrack ever. In its first 11 weeks, the soundtrack, composed by James Horner, sold more than four million copies worldwide.

337. Considering the amount of room available in *Titanic's* lifeboats (1,178 people) and the number saved (705), there was room for an additional 473 individuals if the lifeboats had been filled to capacity.

338. The discovery of the *Titanic* has yielded answers to several questions that have lingered since the *Titanic* sank, including the argument on whether the *Titanic* broke in two when she sank (she did) and if the *Titanic* can ever be raised (although not completely impossible, it would be difficult and expensive since the bow section is mired beneath 60 feet of mud).

339. The *Carpathia* did not bring back every lifeboat from the *Titanic*. Those retrieved to New York were numbers 1, 2, 3, 5 through 13, and 16.

340. "Such a tragedy! Over 2,000 people on board, plenty of time to get off, but 1,500 persons went down with the ship because there were only 20 lifeboats available, definitely not enough to accommodate every man, woman, and child."—Survivor Ruth Becker Blanchard who was 12 when *Titanic* sank.

341. Due to the *Titanic* disaster and it's huge loss of life, the International Ice Patrol was initiated. Using Hercules C-130 aircraft, the patrol monitors shipping lanes of the North Atlantic for icebergs.

342. The name of the pub band performing in steerage in the 1997 movie *Titanic* is the Santa Monica, California-based Gaelic Storm.

343. *ROV Snoop Dog*, much like the *ROV Jason Jr.* used by Dr. Robert Ballard to explore the *Titanic*, was used extensively to photograph *Titanic* during the filming of the 1997 movie *Titanic*.

344. Senator William Alden Smith at the *Titanic* inquiry: "What is an iceberg composed of?" Fifth Officer Harold Lowe's answer: "Ice, I suppose, sir."

345. Military aide to the President, Major Archibald Butt, an authentic *Titanic* passenger who went down with the ship, plays a major role in Jack Finney's 1995 novel *From Time to Time*, which places a time traveler on board the *Titanic* searching for Butt.

346. Four different ships were commissioned by the White Star Line to recover the dead of the *Titanic*. They only found 328 of the more than 1,500 individuals that perished. Of those 328 bodies, 119 were buried at sea.

347. A $3,000 loss of property claim was filed by Emilio Portaluppi against the White Star Line for an auto-graphed picture of Garibaldi that sank with the big ship.

348. Lawrence Beesley, survivor of the *Titanic*, wrote *The Loss of the Titanic*, considered to be the best eyewit-ness account of the affair.

349. Mrs. George D. Widener, who lost her husband and son on the *Titanic*, erected the Widener Memorial Library in honor of son Henry at Harvard University.

350. Survivors of the *Titanic*, according to the British inquiry, included 57 men, 140 women and six children from the first class; 14 men, 80 women and 24 children from second class; 75 men, 76 women and 27 children from third class; and 192 men and 20 women from the crew. The dead included 118 men and four women from first class; 154 men and 13 women from second class; 387 men, 89 women and 52 children from third class; and 670 men and three women from the crew.

351. The American inquiry into the sinking of the *Titanic* featured 82 witnesses that either played a direct or indirect role in the *Titanic's* short history.

352. For more than 80 years researchers and scientists believed that the *Titanic* was torn open by a 300-foot gash to her starboard side by the iceberg that finalized *Titanic's* fate. Researchers and scientists now know that the gash that sunk the *Titanic* was a mere 12 square feet spread over a 300-foot section.

353. Surviving *Titanic* wireless officer Harold Bride stated in the American inquiry that he was paid $1,000 by *The New York Times* for a first-person interview of the disaster.

354. "I didn't leave the ship, it left me."—Second Officer Lightoller to Senator Smith at the American inquiry.

355. After surviving the *Titanic*, Robert Hitchens, helmsman at the time of the collision with the iceberg, became harbormaster in Cape Town, South Africa.

356. The bodies of first-class passengers recovered from the Atlantic were placed in wooden coffins, while those from second and third class and crew member's bodies were sewn into canvas bags and stored in an ice-filled hold.

357. The Mediterranean-bound *Carpathia* returned to New York and, after unloading *Titanic's* lifeboats at the White Star Line pier, docked at Pier 54 at the foot of West Fourteenth Street and unloaded the *Titanic* survivors.

358. The final figure of survivors totaled 705: 201 in first class, 118 in second class, 179 in third class, and 207 crew.

359. The first *Titanic* passengers to depart the *Carpathia* in New York were the first-class passengers.

360. The American Red Cross received $100,000 from *The New York American* newspaper and the Women's Relief Committee for *Titanic* survivors.

361. The White Star Line commissioned the *Lapland* to return the surviving officers and crew of the *Titanic*. Senator Smith subpoenaed the four surviving officers of the *Titanic* and 27 members of the crew for the American inquiry before they could return to England. The *Lapland* returned the remaining 170 of the *Titanic's* crew.

362. According to the British inquiry, of the 711 survivors of the *Titanic* disaster, 338 were men, 316 were women, and 57 were children. In reality, only 705 individuals were saved instead of the 711 calculated by the British Inquiry. Thus, 1,522 men, women and children perished.

363. The first *Titanic* survivor to be a witness during the American inquiry was White Star Line Chairman J. Bruce Ismay. His valet Richard Fry perished when the ship sank.

364. IFREMER and R.M.S. *Titanic* Inc. salvaged close to 3,600 items from the wreckage of the *Titanic* during three separate missions between 1987–1994.

365. Cloris Leachman played Molly Brown and Helen Mirren played stewardess Mary Sloan in the 1979 TV movie *S.O.S. Titanic*, which also starred David Janssen as John Jacob Astor, Susan St. James, Ian Holm and Harry Andrews.

366. The United States Senate inquiry over the *Titanic* disaster was originated at the Waldorf-Astoria Hotel in New York before moving to Washington, D.C.

367. Eugene Daly, a third-class passenger on the *Titanic*, filed a $50 claim for loss of property for his bagpipes.

368. The majority of the third-class staterooms could accommodate either two or four persons while some accommodated up to 10 people.

369. The American and British inquiries recommended several steps to ensure that a disaster like the *Titanic* never reoccur: passenger liners should carry enough lifeboats for all on board; there should be more uniformed boat drills; wireless operators should be on duty 24 hours a day; and that ships have new and improved watertight compartments.

370. *Jason Junior*, or *J.J.*, is a remotely operated vehicle (ROV) that is attached to *Alvin* by a 250-foot-long tether.

371. *Carpathia* wireless officer Harold Cottam testified at the American inquiry that he received $750 from *The New York Times* for his story of the rescue of the *Titanic* survivors.

372. In July 1986, Dr. Robert Ballard returned to the *Titanic* on the *Atlantis II* with *Alvin* and *Jason Junior.* During the expedition, *Alvin* landed on the *Titanic's* decks, and the lawnmower-size *Jason Junior* was used to explore and photograph the interior and exterior of the *Titanic* that were otherwise unreachable to *Alvin*. During this expedition, Ballard photographed the entire wreck, including the debris field.

373. The only davit still standing on the port side of the *Titanic* is the lifeboat davit that accommodated lifeboat #2, which left the *Titanic* at 1:45 a.m. with only 25 people aboard it, much less then the 40 it could seat.

374. *Titanic* lookout Frederick Fleet, the sailor who spotted the iceberg, spent eight days in Washington giving evidence for the American inquiry.

375. *Atlantic,* a stage play based on the sinking of the *Titanic*, debuted in 1930.

376. When the *Titanic's* dead reached Halifax, they were taken to the Mayflower Curling Rink to be embalmed, tagged, and identified.

377. The body of John Jacob Astor was recovered from the Atlantic Ocean and tagged number 124 at the temporary morgue in Halifax. It was the first body to be claimed and released. He was identified by the initials on his shirt and had $2,440 and 250 pounds in his pockets plus a gold belt buckle, gold watch, gold cufflinks, and a diamond ring on his body.

378. Presidential aide and friend to President Taft, Major Archibald Butt has a bridge named in his honor in his home town, Augusta, Georgia.

379. Using the French research vessel *Le Suroit* and the American research vessel *Knorr,* and with the help of *Argo,* an underwater exploration sled complete with video cameras that can project television pictures to the surface, the French-American joint research team discovered the *Titanic* on September 1, 1985.

380. J. Bruce Ismay, chairman of the White Star Line, retired in 1934. Because of poor circulation, he had his right leg amputated in 1936 and on October 17, 1937, Ismay died from a stroke.

381. The Lord Mayor of London organized the Titanic Relief Fund, which totaled 413,200 pounds or more than $2 million for the survivors of the *Titanic*.

382. *Raise the Titanic!*, the 1980 movie based on the best-selling book by Clive Cussler, cost $56 million to film and starred Jason Robards, Richard Jordan, and Alec Guinness.

383. While testifying during the British inquiry, Second Officer Charles Lightoller answered more than 1,600 questions.

384. Edwina Troutt filed a claim of about $2 for loss of property against the White Star Line after losing a marmalade machine in the sinking of the *Titanic*.

385. At the Titanic Band Memorial Concert on May 15, 1912, in the Albert Hall in London, nearly 500 musicians played to commemorate the bravery of the *Titanic* band members.

386. After the American inquiry, J. Bruce Ismay returned to England on May 11, 1912, aboard the White Star Line's *Adriatic*.

387. The American and British inquiries both concluded that several aspects occurred during the *Titanic* disaster that could have prevented the sinking and the large loss of life: the *Titanic* was going too fast; the lookouts were inadequate or hampered by the lack of binoculars; there was no organization when loading and lowering the lifeboats; the *Californian* was in a position to change the outcome of the *Titanic* disaster.

388. The Roman Catholic dead from the *Titanic* were buried at Mount Olivet in Halifax. The Jewish victims that were recovered from the *Titanic* were buried at the Baron de Hirsch cemetery in Halifax. And non-sectarians were buried at Fairview Cemetery.

389. The Minia was chartered to recover the *Titanic's* victims after the *Mackay-Bennett*. The *Minia* recovered 17 bodies, two of which were buried at sea, while the other 15 were returned to Halifax.

390. The last surviving member of the *Titanic* crew was Sidney Daniels. He died in 1983 in Portsmouth, England.

391. Forty thousand people attended memorial services for Macy's Department Store owner Isidor Straus and his wife Ida.

392. In terms of today's dollar, the damage claims for the loss of the *Titanic* totaled some $176 million. The White Star Line paid out a little more than $4 million to *Titanic* claimants: $3.5 million to British claimants and $664,000 to American claimants. Americans had filed claims totaling $16 million.

393. The British inquiry of the *Titanic* disaster included 25,622 questions and answers and filled 959 pages.

394. "Many waters cannot quench love, neither can the floods drown it."—Inscribed on a memorial to Isidor and Ida Straus in a Bronx Cemetery.

395. Like the bow section, the separated stern section now lies in approximately 45 feet of mud.

396. The *Titanic* rests about 1,000 miles due east of Boston, Massachusetts, on the bottom of the Atlantic at a depth of more than 12,460 feet.

397. A 10-foot bust of Wallace Hartley, bandleader of the *Titanic* and casualty of the disaster, can be found in Colne, England, his birthplace. More than 30,000 mourners attended Hartley's memorial service.

398. The British Investigation into the loss of the *Titanic* began on May 2, 1912, in the Scottish Drill Hall near Buckingham Palace in London. A 20-foot model of the *Titanic* was used during the process.

399. The British inquiry cost the nation of England 20,231 pounds or more than $100,000 to investigate the sinking of the *Titanic*.

400. "To me, this is hallowed ground. It really is a special place. It's a devastated piece of wreckage. You'll never raise it. You'll never want to do anything with it but put a wreath on it—which is what we did."—Robert Ballard who discovered the *Titanic's* resting place.

401. The first *Titanic* survivor to testify during the British inquiry was lookout Archie Jewell.

402. With the aid of Brian Ticehurst of the British Titanic Society, the Titanic Historical Society erected a gravestone at the unmarked grave of Frederick Fleet, the famous lookout who spotted the iceberg that sunk the *Titanic*.

403. New York City's mayor set up a relief fund of $161,000 for the *Titanic* survivors.

404. Originally destroyed during World War II, the musicians' memorial which was originally unveiled April 19, 1913, to honor the musicians who died on the *Titanic*, was duplicated and unveiled on March 7, 1990, at the same place where the original was placed. *Titanic* survivors Eva Hart, Edith Haisman, Millvina Dean, and Bert Dean were all in attendance to recognize the heroism displayed by the *Titanic* musicians.

405. One hundred and twenty-eight of the 328 bodies recovered from the *Titanic* were never identified and buried anonymously.

406. "You must remember that we do not have any too much sleep, and therefore when we sleep we die."—Said by the colorful Fifth Officer of the *Titanic*, Harold Lowe, to Senator Smith during the American inquiry in response to his late arrival on the boat deck, due to the fact that no one attempted to wake him.

407. Fifty-nine of the bodies that were recovered and taken to Halifax, Nova Scotia, were claimed by relatives.

408. William Logan Gwinn, one of the three American postal clerks on the *Titanic*, was supposed to work on the *Philadelphia* but had asked to be transferred to the *Titanic* after learning his wife was ill.

409. The last *Titanic* victim recovered from the Atlantic was a saloon steward named James McGrady, whose body was found in mid-May 1912.

410. On April 15, 1995, the 83rd anniversary of the *Titanic* disaster, the National Maritime Museum in London dedicated a memorial garden to those lost in the *Titanic* tragedy that included a granite marker with a bronze plaque that reads: To Commemorate The Sinking Of R.M.S. *Titanic* on 15th April 1912 And All Those Who Were Lost With Her 15 April 1912.

411. "All this vast tragedy makes me look upon it as a different sort of grave. The ship is its own memorial. Leave it there."—*Titanic* survivor Eva Hart's opinion on whether artifacts should be taken from the *Titanic*, which serves as the final resting place of her father.

412. "I do not think that any reasonably probable action by Captain Lord could have led to a different outcome of the tragedy. This of course does not alter the fact that an attempt should have been made."— Captain James de Coverly, who was deputy chief inspector of marine accidents, reached this conclusion concerning the role the *Californian* and its captain, Stanley Lord, should have played in the *Titanic* tragedy.

413. The *Titanic's* bulkheads carried just 10 feet above the waterline.

414. On September 1, 1985, the *Titanic's* long-lost resting place was discovered at 41°43' 32" N, 49°56' 49" W by a joint French/American team led by Jean-Louis Michel and Robert D. Ballard of the Woods Hole Oceanographic Institution.

415. Alvin, a three-man submarine which performed numerous missions exploring the *Titanic* wreck, has a depth range of over 13,000 feet, just enough to explore the *Titanic* wreck.

416. Although the exact numbers of lives lost on the *Titanic* has been disputed since 1912 (some say 1,503, others 1,513, whereas others say 1,522), at least 1,500 people lost their lives on the *Titanic*.

417. "For now the greatest threat to the *Titanic* clearly comes from man."—Dr. Robert D. Ballard.

418. Second Officer Charles Lightoller, the senior officer to survive the sinking of the *Titanic*, retired in the 1920s to operate a chicken farm. Later Lightoller rescued 131 British soldiers on his yacht the *Sundowner* from the shores of Dunkirk and the invading German army in 1940.

419. There are many statues and memorials to the *Titanic* and its heroes. These include a tribute to *Titanic* engineers in Liverpool, England; a "below decks" memorial at Southampton's Holy Rood Church; a memorial near Belfast City Hall, Ireland; the Titanic Memorial Lighthouse in New York City; a statue to Captain Edward J. Smith in Lichfield, Staffordshire, England; a stone tablet in honor of chief wireless officer John Phillips in his hometown of Godalming, Surrey, England; a fountain dedicated to the Isidor and Ida Straus on Broadway in New York City; the Women's Titanic Memorial in Washington in Washington, D.C.; the Thomas Andrews, Jr. Memorial Hall in his hometown of Comber, Northern Ireland; a fountain in Washington, D.C., is dedicated to the memory of Major Archibald Butt and painter Francis Millet; and a writing prize is given to schoolchildren in Dalbeattie, Scotland, which is named after First Officer William Murdoch.

420. In March 1914 Denver architect Charles Smith began to engineer plans to raise the *Titanic* with the use of electromagnets and a submarine. Inadequate funding halted the project before it began.

421. Stanley Lord, captain of *Californian,* was forced to resign from Leyland Line in August 1912. He went on to work 14 years for the London-based Nitrate Producers Steam Ship Company Ltd. until retiring in 1927.

422. "I'm king of the world."—James Cameron after receiving the Oscar for Best Director for the 1997 film *Titanic* (the same line had been used in the film by its main character Jack Dawson).

423. During an expedition on *Titanic* in 1987, researchers discovered the gold pocketwatch of Thomas Brown. After 75 years at the bottom of the Atlantic, Brown's timepiece was returned to his daughter, Edith Brown Haisman, a survivor who was 16 when the *Titanic* sank.

424. While the *Titanic* was sailing away from Queenstown, Ireland, on its way to New York, Eugene Daly sat on the third-class promenade deck and played *Erin's Lament* to the country that he would never see again.

Titanic Organizations

The Titanic Historical Society, Inc.
PO Box 51053
Indian Orchard, Mass. 01151

Titanic International, Inc.
PO Box 7007
Freehold, New Jersey 07728

The British Titanic Society
PO Box 401
Hope Carr Way
Leigh, Lancaster WN7 3WW

Titanic Society of South Africa
PO Box 256, Crown Mines 2025
Johannesburg, South Africa

The Aukland Titanic Club
c/o The President
13 Watling Street
Mt. Eden, Aukland 4
New Zealand

The Switzerland Titanic Society
c/o Lindi Erni
Postfach 123
CH-8613
Uster 3
Switzerland

Selected References

A Cultural History of the Titanic Disaster, Steven Biel, W.W. Norton, 1996.

The Discovery of the Titanic, Dr. Robert D. Ballard, Madison Press Books, 1987.

"Down Into the Deep." *Time,* Jamie Murphy, August 11, 1986.

Her Name Titanic, Charles Pellegrino, Avon Books, 1988.

"How We Found the *Titanic,*" *National Geographic,* Dr. Robert D. Ballard, December 1985.

"The Insider." *People*, Anne-Marie Otey, March 2, 1998.

James Cameron's Titanic, Ed W. Marsh and James Cameron, HarperPerennial, 1997.

The Last Days of the Titanic, E.E. O'Donnell, Roberts Rinehart, 1997.

The Last Dinner on the Titanic, Rick Archbold and
    Dana McCauley, Hyperion/Madison, 1997.

"A Long Last Look at Titanic." *National Geographic,*
    Dr. Robert D. Ballard, December 1986.

Lost Liners, Dr. Robert D. Ballard and Rick Archbold,
    Hyperion/Madison, 1997.

The Night Lives On, Walter Lord, William Morrow &
    Co., Inc., 1986.

A Night To Remember, Walter Lord, Holt, Rinehart and
    Winston, 1955.

On Board the Titanic, Shelley Tanaka,
    Hyperion/Madison, 1996.

Ocean Liners, Robert Wall, Chartwell Books, Inc.,
    1977.

The Sinking of the Titanic, Bruce M. Caplan, Hara
    Publishing, 1997.

The Story of the Titanic as Told by Its Survivors, Jack
    Winocour, Dover Publications, Inc., 1960.

"Sunken Dreams," *People,* Patrick Rogers, Anne-Marie O'Neill, and Sophfronia Scott Gregory, March 16, 1998.

Titanic, Colonel Archibald Gracie, Academy Chicago Publishers, 1996.

The Titanic: End of a Dream, Wyn Craig Wade, Penguin Books, 1980.

Titanic: The Death and Life of a Legend, Michael Davie, Henry Holt & Co., Inc., 1986.

"The Titanic Remembered," *American History Illustrated,* Edward Oxford, April 1986.

Titanic: Destination Disaster, John P. Eaton and Charles A. Haas, W. W. Norton, 1987.

Titanic, Thomas E. Bonsall, Gallery Books, 1987.

Titanic: An Illustrated History, Don Lynch, Hyperion/Madison, 1992.

Titanic Voices: Memories From the Fateful Voyage, Donald Hyslop, Alastair Forsyth and Sheila Jemima, Southampton City Council, 1994.

The Titanic Conspiracy: Cover-ups and Mysteries of the World's Most Famous Sea Disaster, Robin Gardiner and Dan van der Vat, Citadel Press, 1995.

The Titanic: *The Extraordinary Story of the "Unsinkable" Titanic,* Geoff Tibballs, Carlton Books, 1997.

Titanic: Legacy of the World's Greatest Ocean Liner, Susan Wels, Tehabi Books, Inc., 1997.

Titanic Survivor, Violet Jessop and John Maxtone-Graham, Sheridan House, Inc., 1997.

The Titanic Disaster Hearings: The Official Transcripts of the 1912 Senate Investigation, Tom Kuntz, Pocket Books, 1998.

"The Tragedy of the *Titanic,*" *Life,* Charles Hirshberg, June 1997.

The Tennessean, various issues.

Premium gift books from PREMIUM PRESS AMERICA include:

I'LL BE DOGGONE
CATS OUT OF THE BAG

GREAT AMERICAN CIVIL WAR
GREAT AMERICAN GOLF
GREAT AMERICAN OUTDOORS
GREAT AMERICAN GUIDE TO FINE
    WINES

ANGELS EVERYWHERE
MIRACLES
SNOW ANGELS
POWER OF PRAYER

ABSOLUTELY ALABAMA
AMAZING ARKANSAS
FABULOUS FLORIDA
GORGEOUS GEORGIA
SENSATIONAL SOUTH CAROLINA
TERRIFIC TENNESSEE
TREMENDOUS TEXAS
VINTAGE VIRGINIA

TITANIC TRIVIA
BILL DANCE'S FISHING TIPS
DREAM CATCHERS
AMERICA THE BEAUTIFUL

PREMIUM PRESS AMERICA routinely updates existing titles and frequently adds new topics to its growing line of premium gift books. Books are distributed though gift and specialty shops, and bookstores nationwide. If, for any reason, books are not available in your area, please contact the local distributor listed above or contact the Publisher direct by calling 1-800-891-7323. To see our complete backlist and current books, you can visit our website at www.premiumpressamerica.com. Thank you.